Napoleon

Napoleon

Life, Expeditions and Addresses

Tardell M. Ida
LM Publishers

Among the eminent persons of the nineteenth century, Bonaparte is far the best known and the most powerful; and owes his predominance to the fidelity with which he expresses the tone of thought and belief, the aims of the masses of active and cultivated men.

– Ralph W. Emerson

I.

Napoleon Bonaparte was born at Ajaccio, Corsica, on August 15, 1769, the fourth child of Charles Bonaparte and Lætitia Romolino. He was educated in France at the Royal Military Schools of Brienne and of Paris, and when sixteen years old was appointed second lieutenant in a French artillery regiment. From November, 1785, to May, 1792, he was alternately with his regiment and on leaves of absence in Corsica. Sympathizing with the French Revolution, he attempted to aid the Revolutionary party in Corsica against the party of the Corsican patriot, Paoli, but was defeated, and obliged with his family to fly to France. In October, 1793, he was given command of the artillery at the siege of Toulon, and distinguished himself in the capture of the town. After a year and a half of military service in the south, he returned to Paris, and on the 13th *Vendémiaire* (October 5), 1795, he commanded the troops of the Convention against the sections. This led to his being appointed, in 1796, commander-in-chief of the Army of Italy. He went to his post in March, 1796, and after a series of successful battles drove the Austrians into Mantua. Four attempts to relieve the city were made by the enemy, but failed, and in February, 1797, Wurmser, the Austrian general, surrendered. Bonaparte then drove the rest of the Austrian force from Italy, and in October, 1797, signed the treaty of Campo Formio.

In May, 1798, he undertook the conquest of Egypt. He succeeded in entering the country and taking possession of Cairo and Alexandria, but on August 1, at the Battle of the Nile, the French fleet was destroyed by the English under Nelson. A disastrous expedition into Syria occupied the spring of 1799. On returning to Egypt, Bonaparte received news of political disturbances in France, and leaving the army under Kléber he went to Paris, where, by *the coup d' état* of the 18th and 19th *Brumaire* (November 9 and 10) he became First Consul. During Bonaparte's absence in Egypt, war had again broken out between France and Austria, and the First Consul hurried against the enemy. The Battle of Marengo on June 14, 1800, again drove the Austrians from Italy, and February, 1801, peace was concluded. A treaty with England followed in March, 1802. Napoleon now took hold of the reorganization of France with great energy, but in May, 1803, war again broke out between France and England, and the First Consul made elaborate preparations to invade England. While preparing for invasion he was crowned Emperor of the French on December 2, 1804. Before the plan against England could be carried out, Russia and Austria began hostilities, but the alliance was broken by the victory won by Napoleon at Austerlitz on December 2, 1805, and peace was signed at Presburg. The next year, 1806, there was war with Prussia and Russia. Napoleon won the Battle of Jena, October 14, entered Berlin, October 25, and issued the Berlin Decrees declaring a continental blockade against England on November 21. On February 8, 1807, he fought with the Russians the doubtful Battle of Eylau, and on June 14, the decisive Battle of Friedland. The Peace of Tilsit followed, on July 7.

In 1808 Napoleon attempted to take possession of Spain, but before the conquest was complete Austria declared war. The campaign of Wagram in the spring and summer of 1809 subdued the Austrians. In December of 1809, Napoleon divorced Josephine, by whom he had ceased to hope to have an heir to the throne, and in April, 1810, he married the Austrian Princess, Marie Louise. The next year a son, the King of Rome, was born to them. The alliance between France and Russia was broken in 1812, and Napoleon invaded Russia. The campaign ended in a frightful retreat, the army being practically destroyed. Napoleon hastened to Paris, and by the spring of 1813 had a new force in the field. After successful battles at Lützen, Bautzen, and Dresden, he was routed completely at Leipsic in October. The allies invaded France in January, 1814, and a three months' campaign compelled Paris to capitulate, and Napoleon to abdicate. The treaty with the allies gave the Emperor the island of Elbe for life, and hither he went at once, but in February, 1815, he left the island for France, and was greeted joyfully by the French army and nation. Louis XVIII. was obliged to fly from the country, and Napoleon was restored to the throne. The allies immediately attacked him, and at Waterloo, on June 18, 1815, he was defeated. He again resigned the throne, and on July 15 surrendered to the English, who sent him a captive to St. Helena, where he died on May 5, 1821. Napoleon was buried on the island, but in 1840 his remains were removed to France, and placed in the Invalides.

II

The flash of Napoleon Bonaparte's sword so blinded men in his lifetime, and, indeed, long after, that they were unable to distinguish a second weapon in his hand.

The clearer vision which time and study bring have shown that he used words almost as effectively as the sword, and that throughout his career the address ably supported the military manœuvre.

The first complete demonstration of the elaborate use made by Napoleon of the address was the publication of the gigantic work known as the *"Correspondance de Napoleon."* Though the thirty-two ponderous volumes which form this *magnus opus* appeared nearly forty years ago, it is little known to general readers, its size and cost confining it to special libraries, and its documentary character repelling all but special students.

Yet it is only in these volumes that Napoleon's official life can be traced in detail from Toulon to St. Helena. Every document which he wrote relating to public affairs is—if we may believe the editors—printed in the collection. The number is enormous. When the commission appointed to collect the material began its labors, it found itself obliged to go through *ten thousand* volumes pertaining to Napoleon's life. The archives of Paris yielded forty thousand different documents of which he was the author, and the rulers of Austria, Bavaria, Hesse, Russia, Sardinia, and Wurtemberg sent contributions from their royal records.

Across the pages of the great tomes file the mighty procession of soldiers and generals, priests and cardinals, kings and peoples who, in the twenty years in which Napoleon was the preeminent figure of Europe, fell captive to his charms or his power. Here are the words by which he fired starving armies to battle, bullied obstinate powers to follow his plans, put hope into despot-ridden people, told kings their duties.

In these addresses one traces Napoleon's daily thought, so far as he cared to reveal it to others, watches the development of his plans and follows the gradual enlargement of his power. Nowhere else is there so fine an opportunity to observe the steady unfolding of his ambition for world-mastery, to see how he aspired to rule France, then her neighbors, then Europe, the Orient, America, the Isles of the sea. An especially curious study in connection with that of the evolution of his ambition is that of the methods he followed to enlist men in his stupendous undertakings. Such a study is possible only in the addresses.

The spell he exercised over the army is explained here, partially, at least. It was the custom to post the addresses through-out the ranks where each soldier could see and read them. The men had been accustomed at home to seeing all official communications from the Government to the people placed on the bill-boards, and so read them from habit. But Napoleon's bulletins, if they were posted in a familiar way, had a new character. He addressed the soldiers as if they were comrades, explaining the general situation of the army to them, exhorting them to new efforts and promising them rich rewards.

After a battle he stated the results to them, thus giving them a tacit recognition of their importance. The explanation was one that all understood; it was clear and explicit, and bristled with figures. Your common man grasps numbers. They are the bullets of speech and sink in like lead. When Napoleon rattled a volley of numbers at them — "Soldiers, in fifteen days you have gained six victories, taken twenty-one stands of colors, fifty-five pieces of cannon, and several fortresses, and conquered the richest part of Piedmont. You have made fifteen hundred prisoners, and killed or wounded ten thousand men"—they understood, and glowed with pride.

The phrases with which he praised, condemned, exhorted them, were short, terse, and unforgettable. "You will return to your homes, and your countrymen will say as they point you out, 'He belonged to the Army of Italy.'" Not a man with a spark of pride but remembered those words and dreamed that he walked the village street and heard the whisper following him, "He belonged to the Army of Italy." "Soldiers, from the summit of these pyramids forty centuries look down upon you," he cried in Egypt. The splendid phrase voiced the awe of the army in the shadow of the mysterious monuments, and they charged their dark-faced foes as if in the presence of all the heroes of the past.

The perfect clearness and directness of the addresses is their most striking literary quality. The classic pose affected by writers in Napoleon's day he entirely ignored. He wished those whom he addressed to understand his meaning. If he spoke to the soldier it was to convince him that certain facts were true and to persuade him to adopt certain theories. To do this he put what he wished believed and repeated in so clear a fashion that it could not be mistaken. If both bombast and bathos sometimes characterized his addresses to the army, it was never at the expense of his meaning.

The same lucidity marked all his instructions to the Council of State when it was preparing the

Code of Laws. He would not discuss the laws proposed, in technical and equivocal language, but insisted on translating them into the plainest, most evident terms. When it came to wording the laws, he still declared that they should be kept clear of all obscurities and ambiguities of meaning, so that the most illiterate of the people could comprehend them.

While all of Napoleon's addresses to the army and to the people are imbued with a spirit of comradeship, those to generals, ambassadors, counselors of State, even to the members of his family, are imperious and inflexible in tone. The first impression they produce is that the author knows his own mind and is convinced of his ability to carry out his own plans, that he has no superstitious regard for titles, formalities, even for ties of blood, that he is superior to traditions, and will recognize the authority of no man who does not prove himself the stronger. From the beginning of his career, the audacity of this presumption, this confidence in himself, checked and often stifled opposition. There was, in the high tone of his communications, something which compelled obedience, just as there was something in his bearing which silenced those who met him face to face. Augereau went in to his first interview with Napoleon sneering contemptuously at the idea of an untried commander being sent to the Army of Italy, but he backed out from his presence, pale with dismay. "His first glance crushed me," he cried. In a similar way a first address from Napoleon bewildered and silenced critics and opponents. They were baffled by his apparent candor, by the serious way in which he took himself, and by the complete mastery he had of all the elements in a situation. There seemed to be no fact which had escaped him, no contingency he had not considered. A reading of the addresses shows that much of the impression of strength they produce is due to the fact that the writer has full knowledge of the business in hand. One sees from the way in which he criticizes, asks questions, and advises that he understands his subject. Of course, it is in military matters that it is particularly conspicuous. Here he knows everything, the quality of cloth which ought to be used in a soldier's uniform, the way to make a cannon, the kind of food which the horses should receive. Not only did he know what should be done, but he knew if it was done. His communications to officers are bewildering to a lay reader, because of the intimate knowledge they show of each man's actions, and the attention they give to what seems unimportant details. It is not difficult to understand and to share, in reading them, the superstitious feeling that many of Napoleon's associates had that he was "not as other men," that he had superhuman insight and faculties, else how could he know all, foresee all, do all.

Napoleon's attitude towards his family was as imperious as that towards officers and statesmen. Unquestionably he had a warm affection for his mother and brothers and sisters, and even when a mere boy he always thought of them; yet when money and power came to him he would do nothing for them save on condition that they obey absolutely his will; when he became Emperor this determination was firmer than ever. His refusal to acknowledge Jerome Bonaparte's marriage with Miss Paterson is a familiar example of this. His letters to Louis, as King of Holland, to Joseph, as King of Spain, to Jerome, as King of Westphalia, are marked by an amazing absolutism. "All feelings of State yield to State reasons," he sent word to Joseph. "I recognize as relatives only those who serve me. My fortune is not attached to the name of Bonaparte, but to that of Napoleon." As a rule, however, his letters to his family are as conspicuous for their common sense as for their despotism.

When he reached the point in his career where first as consul and then as Emperor he must direct the framing of a new code of laws for France, must organize schools, beautify the capitol, revive industries, his addresses to the councils and officials charged with the duties, show the same knowledge of the principles involved and the same attention to details which distinguish his military writings.

All of the extraordinary stories of Napoleon's capacity for work, of his teeming brain, his incessant invention, which one finds in the memoirs of his secretaries and associates, are fully justified by his addresses. Take one of the days when he was at the height of his power and note the marvelous range over which his thoughts run. He gives direction for the mobilization of troops and the fortification of a town; inquires of Cambacérès or Portalis the meaning of a law they have under consideration for the new Code, asks them why such a law is necessary, if it existed under Louis XIV, why it should not be worded in this way instead of that; he remembers a general who is compromising himself in a love affair, and counsels him at least to be discreet; he scolds Josephine for extravagance; orders a monument to the last general killed on the field of battle; selects the names to be given to certain new streets and bridges of Paris.

To the end of his career his addresses show the same vigor and range. Even those sent to the inhabitants and authorities of Elbe are as fertile in schemes for improving the island as those addressed to the French people; they show, too, the same attention to detail. At Elbe he even dictated, with ceremonious regard for the forms which become the ruler of a kingdom, the kind of bread to be fed his hunting-dogs.

A study of these addresses shows that he never lost his exuberance of imagination. However tragic his losses, he rebounded at once, and on the very day that he dictated his last address to the French army, June 25, 1815, he wrote his librarian to send him all the books on the United States which were to be obtained. He wanted to study up the country which he had already chosen for his future home.

Even at St. Helena, sick and irritated as he was, his mind was never quiet. He dictated in the five and a half years he lived on the island most of the matter in the journals of O'Meara, Las Cases, and Montholon, his essays on Cæsar, Turenne, and Frederick, his commentaries and several less important works, — a respectable literary output, certainly, for five and a half years, and an excellent reply to the old charge that the fallen Emperor passed his imprisonment sulking.

It is because the addresses of Napoleon are so characteristic of the man, because they reveal so clearly his ambitions, his methods, his genius and his faults, that this selection from them is offered to the public. It is a sketch of Napoleon by himself; an incomplete sketch, to be sure, but one in which every bold, sharp line is by his own hand.

III
THE CAMPAIGN IN ITALY

Address to the Army at the Beginning of the Campaign, March, 1796.

"Soldiers, you are naked and ill-fed! Government owes you much and can give you nothing. The patience and courage you have shown in the midst of these rocks are admirable; but they gain you no renown; no glory results to you from your endurance. It is my design to lead you into the most fertile plains of the world. Rich provinces and great cities will be in your power; there you will find honor, glory, and wealth. Soldiers of Italy! will you be wanting in courage or perseverance?"

Proclamation to the Army, May, 1796.

"Soldiers: You have in fifteen days gained six victories, taken twenty-one stand of colors, fifty-five pieces of cannon, and several fortresses, and overrun the richest part of Piedmont; you have made 15,000 prisoners, and killed or wounded upwards of 10,000 men. Hitherto you have been fighting for barren rocks, made memorable by your valor, though useless to your country, but your exploits now equal those of the Armies of Holland and the Rhine. You were utterly destitute, and you have supplied all your wants. You have gained battles without cannon, passed rivers without bridges, performed forced marches without shoes, and bivouacked without strong liquors, and often without bread. None but Republican phalanxes, the soldiers of liberty, could have endured what you have done; thanks to you, soldiers, for your perseverance!

Your grateful country owes its safety to you; and if the taking of Toulon was an earnest of the immortal campaign of 1794, your present victories foretell one more glorious. The two armies which lately attacked you in full confidence, now fly before you in consternation; the perverse men who laughed at your distress, and inwardly rejoiced at the triumph of your enemies, are now confounded and trembling. But, soldiers, you have yet done nothing, for there still remains much to do. Neither Turin nor Milan are yours; the ashes of the conquerors of Tarquin are still trodden underfoot by the assassins of Basseville. It is said that there are some among you whose courage is shaken, and who would prefer returning to the summits of the Alps and Apennines. No, I cannot believe it. The victors of Montenotte, Millesimo, Dego, and

Mondovi are eager to extend the glory of the French name!"

Letter to "The Directory."
"Headquarters, Lodi",
May 11, 1796

"*Citizen Directors:*—I thought that the passage of the Po would be the most audacious performance of the campaign, the Battle of Millesimo the liveliest encounter, but I have yet to give you an account of the Battle of Lodi.

"At three o'clock on the morning of the 21st, we pitched our headquarters at Casal. At nine o'clock, our vanguard encountered the enemy defending the approaches to Lodi. I immediately ordered all the cavalry to mount with four pieces of light artillery which had just arrived, drawn by the carriage horses of the lords of Plaisance.

"The division of General Augereau, which had camped overnight at Borghetto, and that of General Massena, which slept at Casal, were put in motion. Meantime, our vanguard had overturned all the posts of the enemy, and seized one of their cannon. We pursued the enemy into Lodi, they having already crossed the Adda by the bridge. Beaulieu with all his army was drawn up in battle array.

Thirty set cannon defended the passage of the bridge. I formed all my artillery into a battery. The cannonading was very lively for several hours.

"As soon as the army arrived it formed into a close column with the second battalion of rifles at its head, followed by all the battalions of grenadiers. On the run, with cries of *Vive la République*, they appeared on the bridge, which is over six hundred feet long. The enemy kept up a terrible fire. The head of the column almost seemed to waver. A moment's hesitation and all would have been lost. The Generals Berthier, Masséna, Cervoni, Dallemagne, the Brigadier-General Lannes, and Battalion-Commander Dupas felt this, and, rushing to the front, decided the fate of the day.

"This redoubtable column overrode all opposition, breaking Beaulieu's order of battle, capturing all his artillery, and sowing on all sides seeds of terror, flight, and death. In the twinkling of an eye the enemy's army was dispersed. The Generals Rusca, Augereau, and Beyrand crossed as soon as their divisions arrived, and completed the victory. The cavalry crossed the Adda at a ford; but the ford proving extremely bad, there was much delay, which prevented an engagement.

"The enemy's cavalry tried charging our troops, in order to protect the retreat of their infantry, but our men were hard to frighten.

"Nightfall and the extreme fatigue of the troops, many of whom had made more than ten leagues during the day, forced us to forego the pleasure of pursuit.

"The enemy lost twenty pieces of cannon, and from two to three thousand killed, wounded or prisoners. We lost but 150 men, dead and wounded.

"Citizen Latour, General Masséna's captain aide-de-camp, received several sabre cuts. I want the place of battalion commander for this brave officer.

"Citizen Marmont, my aide-de-camp brigadier-general, had a horse shot under him.

"Citizen Lemarois, my captain aide-de-camp, had his clothes riddled by balls. The courage of this young officer is equal to his activity.

"If called upon to name all the soldiers who distinguished themselves on that extraordinary day, I should be obliged to name all the riflemen and grenadiers of the vanguard, and nearly all the officers of the staff. But I must not forget the intrepid Berthier, who was, in one day, gunner, cavalier, and grenadier. Brigadier-General Sugny, commanding the artillery, conducted himself creditably.

"Beaulieu fled with the remains of his army. Already Normandy may be considered as belonging to the Republic. At this moment Beaulieu is passing through the Venetian States, many of whose cities have closed their doors upon him.

"I hope soon to send you the keys of Milan and Pavia.

"Although, since the beginning of the campaign, we have had some pretty hot encounters, which the army of the French Republic have met with audacity, not one of them has approached the terrible passage of the bridge at Lodi.

"If we have lost but few men it is due to promptness of execution, and to the sudden effect produced upon the opposing army by the size and formidable fire of our intrepid column."

Letter to "The Directory."

"Headquarters, Lodi",

May 14, 1796

"*Citizen Directors*:—I think it most impolitic to divide the Italian army into two sections; it is equally contrary to the interests of the Republic to put two generals in command.

"The expedition against Livourne, Rome, and Naples is a small affair; it can be accomplished by arranging the divisions in echelon in such a manner as to enable them, by a retrograde march, to appear in force against the Austrians, and threaten to hem them in at the slightest movement on their part.

"For this it is not only necessary to have one general, but he should have nothing to hinder him in his march or in his operations. I have conducted the campaign without consulting any one. I should have accomplished nothing worth the trouble had I been obliged to reconcile my ideas with those of another. I have gained some advantages over very superior forces while in an almost destitute condition; because I was persuaded of your entire confidence in me, my moves were as prompt as my thoughts.

"If you fetter me on all sides; if it is necessary for me to confer with the commissioners of the Government regarding each step; if they have the right to change my movements, to send me troops or withdraw them at their will, then look for no good.

"If you reduce your power by dividing your forces, if you break the unity of the military outline in Italy, with grief I tell you, you will have lost the most favorable occasion for bringing Italy to terms.

"In the present condition of the affairs of the Republic in Italy, it is indispensable for you to have a general in whom you have entire confidence. If it is not I, I make no complaint, I shall only strive to redouble my zeal in order to merit your esteem in the past that you may confide to me. Everyone has his own manner of conducting a war. General Keelerman has had more experience and will do better than I, but together we would make a dire failure.

"I cannot render our country any essential service unless invested with your absolute and entire confidence. It requires much courage on my part to write you in this way, I could so easily be accused of pride and ambition. But I owe the expression of all my opinions on the subject to one whose many tokens of esteem I shall never forget."

Proclamation to the Soldiers on Entering Milan, May 15, 1796.

"Soldiers: You have rushed like a torrent from the top of the Apennines; you have overthrown and scattered all that opposed your march. Piedmont, delivered from Austrian tyranny, indulges her natural sentiments of peace and friendship towards France. Milan is yours, and the Republican flag waves throughout Lombardy. The Dukes of Parma and Modena owe their political existence to your generosity alone. The army which so proudly threatened you can find no barrier to protect it against your courage; neither the Po, the Ticino, nor the Adda could stop you for a single day. These vaunted bulwarks of Italy opposed you in vain; you passed them as rapidly as the Apennines. These great successes have filled the heart of your country with joy. Your representatives have ordered a festival to commemorate your victories, which has been held in every district of the Republic. There your fathers, your mothers, your wives, sisters, and mistresses rejoiced in your good fortune, and proudly boasted of belonging to you. Yes, soldiers, you have done much,—but remains there nothing more to do? Shall it be said of us that we knew how to conquer, but not how to make use of victory? Shall posterity reproach us with having found Capau in Lombardy? But I see you already hasten to arms. An effeminate repose is tedious to you; the days which are lost to glory are lost to your happiness. Well, then, let us set forth! We have still forced marches to make, enemies to subdue, laurels to gather, injuries to revenge. Let those who have sharpened the daggers of civil war in France, who have basely murdered our ministers, and burnt our ships at Toulon, tremble! The hour of vengeance has struck; but let the people of all countries be free from apprehension; we are the friends of the people everywhere, and those great men whom we have taken for our models. To restore the capitol, to replace the statues of the heroes who rendered it illustrious, to rouse the Roman people, stupefied by several ages of slavery,—such will be the fruit of our victories; they will form an era for posterity; you will have the immortal glory of changing the face of the finest part of Europe. The French people, free and respected by the whole world, will give to Europe a glorious peace, which will indemnify them for the sacrifices of every kind which for the last six years they have been making. You will then return to your homes and your country. Men will say as they point you out, '*He belonged to the army of Italy.*'"

Proclamation to the Troops on Entering Brescia, May 28, 1796.

"It is to deliver the finest country in Europe from the iron yoke of the proud House of Austria, that the French army has braved the most formidable obstacles. Victory, siding with justice, has crowned its efforts with success, the wreck of the enemy's army has retreated behind the Mincio. In order to pursue them, the French army enters the territory of the Republic of Venice; but it will not forget that the two Republics are united by ancient friendship. Religion, government, and customs shall be respected. Let the people be free from apprehension, the severest discipline will be kept up; whatever the army is supplied with shall be punctually paid for in money. The general-in-chief invites the officers of the Republic of Venice, the magistrates, and priests to make known his sentiments to the people, in order that the friendship which has so long subsisted between the two nations may be cemented by confidence. Faithful in the path of honor as in that of victory, the French soldier is terrible only to the enemies of his liberty and his Government."

Address to Soldiers During the Siege of Mantua, Nov. 6, 1796.

"Soldiers: I am not satisfied with you; you have shown neither bravery, discipline, nor perseverance; no position could rally you; you abandoned yourselves to a panic-terror; you suffered yourselves to be driven from situations where a handful of brave men might have stopped an army. Soldiers of the 39th and 85th, you are not

French soldiers. Quartermaster-general, let it be inscribed on their colors, '*They no longer form part of the Army of Italy!*'"

Address to the Troops on the Conclusion of the First Italian Campaign, March, 1797.

"Soldiers: The campaign just ended has given you imperishable renown. You have been victorious in fourteen pitched battles and seventy actions. You have taken more than a hundred thousand prisoners, five hundred field-pieces, two thousand heavy guns, and four pontoon trains. You have maintained the army during the whole campaign. In addition to this, you have sent six millions of dollars to the public treasury, and have enriched the National Museum with three hundred masterpieces of the arts of ancient and modern Italy, which it has required thirty centuries to produce. You have conquered the finest countries in Europe. The French flag waves for the first time upon the Adriatic opposite to Macedon, the native country of Alexander. Still higher destinies await you. I know that you will not prove unworthy of them. Of all the foes that conspired to stifle the Republic in its birth, the Austrian Emperor alone remains before you. To obtain peace we must seek it in the heart of his hereditary State. You will there find a brave people, whose religion and customs you will respect, and whose prosperity you will hold sacred. Remember that it is liberty you carry to the brave Hungarian nation."

Address to the Genoese, 1797.

"I will respond, citizens, to the confidence you have reposed in me. It is not enough that you refrain from hostility to religion. You should do nothing which can cause inquietude to tender consciences. To exclude the nobles from any public office, is an act of extreme injustice. You thus repeat the wrong which you condemn in them. Why are you people of Genoa so changed? Their first impulses of fraternal kindness have been succeeded by terror and fear. Remember that the priests were the first who rallied around the tree of liberty. They first told you that the morality of the gospel is democratic. Men have taken advantage of the faults, perhaps of the crimes of individual priests, to unite against Christianity. You have proscribed without discrimination. When a State becomes accustomed to condemn without hearing, to applaud a discourse because it is impassioned; when exaggeration and madness are called virtue, moderation and equity designated as crimes, that State is near its ruin. Believe me, I shall consider that one of the happiest moments of my life in which I hear that the people of Genoa are united among themselves and live happily."

Extract from a Letter to the Directory, April, 1797.

"From these different posts we shall command the Mediterranean, we shall keep an eye on the Ottoman Empire, which is crumbling to pieces, and we shall have it in our power to render the dominion of the ocean almost useless to the English. They have possession of the Cape of Good Hope. We can do without it. *Let us occupy Egypt.* We shall be in the direct road for India. It will be easy for us to found there one of the finest colonies in the world. *It is in Egypt that we must attack England.*"

Address to Soldiers after the Signing of the Treaty of Campo Formio, October, 1797.

"Soldiers: I set out to-morrow for Germany. Separated from the army, I shall sigh for the moment of my rejoining it, and brave fresh dangers. Whatever post Government may assign to the soldiers of the Army of Italy, they will always be the worthy supporters of liberty and of the glory of the French name. Soldiers, when you talk of the Princes you have conquered, of the nations you have set free, and the battles you have fought in two campaigns, say: *In the next two we shall do still more!*"

Proclamation to the Cisalpine Republic, Nov. 17, 1797.

"We have given you liberty. Take care you preserve it. To be worthy of your destiny make only discreet and honorable laws, and cause them to be executed with energy. Favor the diffusion of knowledge, and respect religion. Compose your battalions not of disreputable men, but with citizens imbued with the principles of the Republic, and closely linked with the prosperity. You have need to impress yourselves with the feelings of your strength, and with the dignity which befits the free man. Divided and bowed by ages of tyranny, you could not alone have achieved your independence. In a few years, if true to yourselves, no nation will be strong enough to wrest liberty from you. Till then the great nation will protect you."

Proclamation on Leaving the Troops at Rastadt, November, 1797.

"Soldiers: I leave you to-morrow. In separating myself from the army I am consoled with the thought that I shall soon meet you again, and engage with you in new enterprises. Soldiers, when conversing among yourselves of the kings you have vanquished, of the people upon whom you have conferred liberty, of the victories you have won in two campaigns, say, 'In the next two we will accomplish still more.'"

Address to the Citizens after the Signing of the Treaty of Campo Formio, Dec. 10, 1787.

"Citizens: The French people, in order to be free, had kings to combat. To obtain a constitution founded on reason it had the prejudices of eighteen centuries to overcome. Priestcraft, feudalism, despotism, have successively, for two thousand years, governed Europe. From the peace you have just concluded dates the era of representative governments. You have succeeded in organizing the great nation, whose vast territory is circumscribed only because nature herself has fixed its limits. You have done more. The two finest countries in Europe, formerly as renowned for the arts, the sciences, and the illustrious men, whose cradle they were, see with the greatest hopes genius and freedom issuing from the tomb of their ancestors. I have the honor to deliver to you the treaty signed at Campo Formio, and ratified by the Emperor. Peace secures the liberty, the prosperity, and the glory of the Republic. As soon as the happiness of France is secured by the best organic laws, the whole of Europe will be free."

IV

THE EGYPTIAN EXPEDITION.

Proclamation to the Troops on Entering Toulon, May 9, 1798.

"Soldiers: You are one of the wings of the Army of England. You have made war in mountains, plains, and cities. It remains to make it on the ocean. The Roman legions, whom you have often imitated, but never yet equaled, combated Carthage, by turns, on the seas and on the plains of Zama. Victory never deserted their standards, because they never ceased to be brave, patient, and united. Soldiers, the eyes of Europe are upon you. You have great destinies to accomplish, battles to fight, dangers and fatigues to overcome. You are about to do more than you have yet done, for the prosperity of your country, the happiness of man, and for your own glory."

Address to the Military Commissioners, May 16, 1798.

"BONAPARTE, MEMBER OF THE NATIONAL INSTITUTE, TO THE MILITARY COMMISSIONERS OF THE NINTH DIVISION, ESTABLISHED BY THE LAW OF THE 19TH FRUCTIDOR.

"I have learned, citizens, with deep regret, that an old man, between seventy and eighty years of age, and some unfortunate women, in a state of pregnancy, or surrounded by children of tender age, have been shot on the charge of emigration.

"Have the soldiers of liberty become executioners? Can the mercy which they have exercised even in the fury of the battle be extinct in their hearts?

"The law of the 19th Fructidor was a measure of public safety. Its object was to reach conspirators, not women and aged men.

"I therefore exhort you, citizens, whenever the law brings to your tribunals women or old men, to declare that in the field of battle you have respected the women and old men of your enemies.

"The officer who signs a sentence against a person incapable of bearing arms is a coward."

Proclamation to the Troops on Embarking for E Egypt, June, 1798

"BONAPARTE, MEMBER OF THE NATIONAL

"the 4th Messidor, year 6.
INSTITUTE, GENERAL-IN-CHIEF.
"HEADQUARTERS ON BOARD THE *Orient*,

"*Soldiers:*—You are about to undertake a conquest the effects of which, on civilization and commerce, are incalculable. The blow you are about to give to England will be the best aimed, the most sensibly felt, she can receive until the time arrives when you can give her her death-blow.

"We must make some fatiguing marches; we must fight several battles; we shall succeed in all we undertake. The destinies are with us. The Mameluke beys, who favor exclusively English commerce, whose extortions oppress our merchants, and who tyrannize over the unfortunate inhabitants of the Nile, a few days after our arrival will no longer exist.

"The people amongst whom we are going to live are Mahometans. The first article of their faith is this: 'There is but one God and Mahomet is His prophet.' Do not contradict them, Behave to them as you behaved to the Jews—to the Italians. Pay respect to their muftis and their imaums, as you did to the rabbis and the bishops. Extend to the ceremonies prescribed by the Koran and the mosques the same toleration which you showed to the synagogues, to the religion of Moses and of Jesus Christ.

"The Roman legions protect all religions. You will here find customs different from those of Europe. You must accommodate yourselves to them. The people amongst whom we are about to mix differ from us in the treatment of women; but in all countries he who violates is a monster. Pillage only enriches a small number of men; it dishonors us; it destroys our resources; it converts into enemies the people whom it is our interest to have for friends.

"The first town we shall come to was built by Alexander. At every step we shall meet with grand recollections, worthy of exciting the emulation of Frenchmen."

Proclamation to the Egyptians, July, 1798.

"People of Egypt: You will be told by our enemies, that I am come to destroy your religion.

Believe them not. Tell them that I am come to restore your rights, punish your usurpers, and raise the true worship of Mahomet. Tell them that I venerate, more than I do the Mamelukes, God, His prophet, and the Koran. Tell them that all men are equal in the sight of God; that wisdom, talents, and virtue alone constitute the difference between them. And what are the virtues which distinguish the Mamelukes, that entitle them to appropriate all the enjoyments of life to themselves? If Egypt is their farm, let them show their lease, from God, by which they hold it. Is there a fine estate? It belongs to the Mamelukes. Is there a beautiful slave, a fine horse, a good house? All belong to the Mamelukes. But God is just and merciful, and He hath ordained that the Empire of the Mamelukes shall come to an end. Thrice happy those who shall side with us; they shall prosper in their fortune and their rank. Happy they who shall be neutral; they will have time to become acquainted with us, and will range themselves upon our side. But woe, threefold woe, to those who shall arm for the Mamelukes and fight against us! For them there will be no hope; they shall perish."

Letter to "The Directory."

"HEADQUARTERS, CAIRO"

6 Thermidor, year 4. (24 July, 1798.)

"*Citizen Directors:*—On the morning of the 2d Thermidor we caught sight of the Pyramids.

"On the evening of the 2d, we were within six leagues of Cairo, and I learned that the twenty-three beys, with all their forces, were intrenched at Embâbeh, and that their intrenchments were armed by more than sixty pieces of cannon.

"BATTLE OF THE PYRAMIDS."

On the 3d, at dawn, we encountered their vanguard, which we drove from village to village. At 2 o'clock in the afternoon we arrived before their intrenchments and found ourselves in the presence of the enemy.

"I ordered the divisions of Generals Desaix and Reynier to take up their position on the right, between Gyseh and Embâbeh, in such a manner as to cut off the enemy's communication with upper Egypt, which is their natural retreat. The position of the army was the same as at Battle of Chobiâkhyt.

"No sooner had Mourad-Bey perceived General Desaix's movements, than he resolved to charge him. He despatched one of his bravest beys with a corps of picked men, who, with lightning rapidity, charged the two divisions. They were allowed to get within fifty feet, then we greeted them with a shower of balls and grape-shot which left many of their number dead on the battle-field. They dashed into the space formed by the two divisions, where they were received by a double fire which completed their defeat.

"I seized the opportunity and ordered General Bon's division, which was on the Nile, to prepare for an attack on the enemy's intrenchments. I ordered General Menon's division, which was commanded by General Vial, to bear down between the corps that had just charged us and the intrenchments, in such a manner as to accomplish the triple end of,—

"Preventing this corps reëntering their intrenchments.

"Cutting off the retreat of those who occupied them.

"And finally, if necessary, of attacking the intrenchments on the left.

"Directly the generals, Vial and Bon, were in position, they ordered the first and third divisions of each battalion to draw up in columns of attack, while the second and fourth retained their former position, forming a square battalion, now only three deep, while they advanced to support the columns of attack.

"General Bon's columns of attack, commanded by the brave General Rampon, threw themselves upon the intrenchments with their usual impetuosity, in spite of the fire from a large quantity of artillery, when suddenly the Mamelukes made a charge. They emerged from their intrenchments on a full gallop, but our columns had time to come to a halt, to face all sides, and receive them on the points of their bayonets, or by a shower of balls. In an instant the field was strewn with the enemy.

"Our troops soon razed their intrenchments. The Mamelukes fled, precipitating themselves *en masse* upon their left, but General Vial was ready for them. They were obliged to pass within five feet of a battalion of our riflemen, and the butchery was awful. A large number threw themselves into the Nile and were drowned.

"After the numerous combats and battles that my troops have gained over superior forces, I should not think of praising their conduct and their *sang-froid* on this occasion, were it not that this new method of warfare has required, on their part, a patience which contrasts with French impetuosity. Had they given way to their ardor they could not have gained the victory, which was obtainable only by great coolness and patience.

"The Mamelukes' cavalry displayed great bravery; they defended their fortunes, and upon every one of them our soldiers found from three to five hundred louis.

"All the luxury of these people is in their horses and their accoutrements; their houses are pitiable.

"It would be difficult to find a land more fertile, and a people more miserable, more ignorant, more abject. They prefer one of our soldier's buttons to a six-franc piece.

"In the villages they do not even know the sight of a pair of scissors. Their houses are made of a little mud. Their sole furniture is a mat of straw and two or three earthen pots. They eat and burn very little as a general thing. They do not know the use of mills; consequently, we frequently bivouacked on stalks of wheat without being able to obtain any flour. We live on vegetables and cattle. The little grain they do use, they grind into flour with stones, and in some of the large villages they have mills turned by oxen.

"We are constantly annoyed by clouds of Arabs; they are the greatest robbers and the greatest rascals on the face of the earth, assassinating alike Turks and French, or anyone who falls in their way.

"Brigadier-General Mireur and several aides-de-camp and officers of the staff have been assassinated by these wretches. They lie in ambush behind banks and ditches on their excellent little horses, and woe to him who ventures to wander a hundred feet from the columns.

"By a fatality that I have often observed to follow men whose last hour approaches. General Mireur went alone, in spite of the remonstrances of the main-guard, to a little elevation about two hundred feet from the camp. Behind it were stationed three Bedouins who murdered him.

"The Republic has met with a real loss. He was one of the bravest generals I have ever known.

"There is very little coin in this country, not enough to pay the army. There is plenty of wheat, rice, vegetables, and cattle. The Republic could not have a colony better suited to its needs, nor of a richer soil. The climate is very healthy, owing to the cool nights.

"In spite of fifteen days' march, and all kinds of fatigue, the absolute deprivation of wine, in fact, of everything that could alleviate fatigue, we have no one on the sick list. The soldiers have found a great resource in the *postèques*, a kind of watermelon that is very abundant here."

Order Respecting the Government of Egypt, July 27, 1798.

"Headquarters, Cairo",

9th Thermidol, year 6.

"Bonaparte, Member of the National Institute, General-in-Chief, Orders:

"Article I. There shall be in each province of Egypt a divan, composed of seven individuals, whose duty it will be to superintend the interests of the province; to communicate to me any complaints that may be made; to prevent warfare among the different villages; to apprehend and punish criminals (for which purpose they may demand assistance from the French commandant); and to take every opportunity of enlightening the people.

"Art. II. There shall be in each province an aga of the Janizaries, maintaining constant communication with the French commandant. He shall have with him a company of sixty armed natives, whom he may take wherever he pleases, for the maintenance of good order, subordination, and tranquillity.

"Art. III. There shall be in each province an intendant, whose business will be to levy the Miri, the feddan, and the other contributions which formerly belonged to the Mamelukes, but which now belong to the French Republic. The intendants shall have as many agents as may be necessary.

"ART. IV. The said intendant shall have a French agent to correspond with the Finance Department, and to execute all the orders he may receive."

Letter to Tippoo Saib, Jan. 25, 1799.

"You are, of course, already informed of my arrival on the banks of the Red Sea, with a numerous and invincible army. Eager to deliver you from the iron yoke of England, I hasten to request that you will send me, by the way of Muscate or Mocha, an account of the political situation in which you are. I also wish that you would send to Suez, or Grand Cairo, some able man, in your confidence, with whom I may confer."

Proclamation to the Army, on the Abandoning of the Siege of Acre, May, 1799.

"Soldiers: You have traversed the desert which separates Asia from Africa, with the rapidity of an Arab force. The army, which was on its march to invade Egypt, is destroyed. You have taken its general, its field-artillery, camels, and baggage.

You have captured all the fortified posts, which secure the wells of the desert. You have dispersed, at Mount Tabor, those swarms of brigands, collected from all parts of Asia, hoping to share the plunder of Egypt. The thirty ships, which twelve days since you saw enter the port of Acre, were destined for an attack upon Alexandria. But you compelled them to hasten to the relief of Acre. Several of their standards will contribute to adorn your triumphal entry into Egypt. After having maintained the war with a handful of men, during three months, in the heart of Syria, taken forty pieces of cannon, fifty stands of colors, six thousand prisoners, and captured or destroyed the fortifications of Gaza, Jaffa, and Acre, we prepare to return to Egypt, where, by a threatened invasion, our presence is imperiously demanded. A few days longer might give you the hope of taking the Pacha in his palace. But at this season the palace of Acre is not worth the loss of three days, nor the loss of those brave soldiers who would consequently fall, and who are necessary for more essential services. Soldiers, we have yet a toilsome and a perilous task to perform. After having by this campaign secured ourselves from attacks from the eastward, it will perhaps be necessary to repel the efforts which may be made from the west."

Proclamation to the Army on his Departure for France, August, 1799.

"The news from Europe has determined me to proceed to France. I leave the command of the army to General Kléber. The army shall hear from me forthwith; at present I can say no more. It costs me much pain to quit troops to whom I am so strongly attached. But my absence will be but temporary, and the general I leave in command has the confidence of the Government as well as mine."

V
NAPOLEON, FIRST CONSUL.

Proclamation to the French People, Nov. 10, 1799.

19th Brumaire, 11 o'clock, P. M.

"Frenchmen: On my return to France I found division reigning amongst all the authorities. They agreed only on this single point, that the Constitution was half destroyed, and was unable to protect liberty.

"Each party in turn came to me, confided to me their designs, imparted their secrets, and requested my support. I refused to be the man of a party.

"The Council of the Ancients appealed to me. I answered their appeal. A plan of general restoration had been concerted by men whom the nation has been accustomed to regard as the defenders of liberty, equality, and property. This plan required calm and free deliberation, exempt from all influence and all fear. The Ancients resolved, therefore, upon the removal of the legislative bodies to St. Cloud. They placed at my disposal the force necessary to secure their independence. I was bound, in duty to my fellow citizens, to the soldiers perishing in our armies, and to the national glory, acquired at the cost of so much blood, to accept the command.

"The councils assembled at St. Cloud. Republican troops guaranteed their safety from without, but assassins created terror within. Many members of the Council of the Five Hundred, armed with stilettos and pistols, spread menaces of death around them.

"The plans which ought to have been developed were withheld. The majority of the council was rendered inefficient; the boldest orators were disconcerted, and the inutility of submitting any salutary proposition was quite evident.

"I proceeded, filled with indignation and grief, to the Council of the Ancients. I besought them to carry their noble designs into execution. I directed their attention to the evils of the nation, which were their motives for conceiving those designs. They concurred in giving me new proofs of their uniform good-will.

"I presented myself before the Council of the Five Hundred, alone, unarmed, my head uncovered, just as the Ancients had received and applauded me. My object was to restore to the majority the expression of its will, and to secure to it its power.

"The stilettos which had menaced the deputies were instantly raised against their deliverer. Twenty assassins rushed upon me, and aimed at my breast. The grenadiers of the legislative body, whom I had left at the door of the hall, ran forward, and placed themselves between me and the assassins. One of these brave grenadiers (Thomé) had his clothes pierced by a stiletto. They bore me off.

"At the same moment cries of 'Outlaw him' were raised against the defender of the law. It was the horrid cry of assassins against the power destined to repress them.

"They crowded around the President, uttering threats. With arms in their hands they commanded him to declare 'the outlawry.' I was informed of this. I ordered him to be rescued from their fury, and six grenadiers of the legislative body brought him out. Immediately afterwards some grenadiers of the legislative body charged into the hall and cleared it.

"The factions, intimidated, dispersed and fled. The majority, freed from their assaults, returned freely and peaceably into the hall, listened to the propositions made for the public safety, deliberated, and drew up the salutary resolution which will become the new and provisional law of the Republic.

"Frenchmen, you doubtless recognize in this conduct the zeal of a soldier of liberty, of a citizen devoted to the Republic. Conservative, tutelary, and liberal ideas resumed their authority upon the dispersion of the factions, who domineered in the councils, and who, in rendering themselves the most odious of men, did not cease to be the most contemptible."

Proclamation to the Army of the East, November, 1799.

"Soldiers: The Consuls of the French Republic frequently direct their attention to the Army of the East.

"France acknowledged all the influence of your conquests on the restoration of her trade and civilization of the world.

"The eyes of all Europe are upon you, and in thought I am often with you.

"In whatsoever situation the chances of war may place you, prove yourselves still the soldiers of Rivoli and Aboukir—you will be invincible.

"Place in Kléber the boundless confidence you placed in me. He deserves it.

"Soldiers, think of the day when you will return victorious to the sacred territory of France. That will be a glorious day for this whole nation."

Proclamation to the French before the Second Italian Campaign.

"Frenchmen: You have been anxious for peace. Your Government has desired it with still greater ardor. Its first efforts, its constant wishes, have been for its attainment. The English Ministry has exposed the secret of its iniquitous policy. It wishes to dismember France, to destroy its commerce, and either to erase it from the map of Europe, or to degrade it to a secondary power. England is willing to embroil all the nations of the Continent in hostility with each other, that she may enrich herself with the spoils, and gain possession of the trade of the world. For the attainment of this object she scatters her gold, becomes prodigal of her promises, and multiplies her intrigues."

Proclamation to the Soldiers before the Battle of Marengo, June, 1800.

"Soldiers: When we began our march, one department of France was in the hands of the enemy. Consternation pervaded the south of the Republic. You advanced. Joy and hope in our country have succeeded to consternation and fear. The enemy, terror-struck, seeks only to regain his frontiers. You have taken his hospitals, his magazines, his reserve parks. The first act of the campaign is finished. Millions of men address you in strains of praise. But shall we allow our audacious enemies to violate with impunity the territory of the Republic? Will you permit the army to escape which has carried terror into your families? You will not. March, then, to meet him. Tear from his brows the laurels he has won. Teach the world that a malediction attends those that violate the territory of the Great People. The result of our efforts will be unclouded glory, and a durable peace."

Letter to the Emperor of Austria, on the Field of Marengo, June, 1800.

"*Sire:*—It is on the field of battle, amid the sufferings of a multitude of wounded, and surrounded by fifteen thousand corpses, that I beseech your Majesty to listen to the voice of humanity, and not to suffer two brave nations to cut each other's throats for interests not their own. It is my part to press this upon your Majesty, being upon the very theatre of war. Your Majesty's heart cannot feel it so keenly as does mine.

"For what are you fighting? For religion? Then make war on the Russians and the English, who are the enemies of your faith. Do you wish to guard against revolutionary principles? It is this very war which has extended them over half the continent, by extending the conquests of France. The continuance of the war cannot fail to diffuse them still further. Is it for the balance of Europe? The English threaten that balance far more than does France, for they have become the masters and the tyrants of commerce, and are beyond the reach of resistance. Is it to secure the interests of the House of Austria? Let us then execute the Treaty of Campo Formio, which secures to your Majesty large indemnities in compensation for the provinces lost in the Netherlands, and secures them to you where you most wish to obtain them, that is, in Italy. Your Majesty may send negotiators whither you will, and we will add to the Treaty of Campo Formio stipulations calculated to assure you of the continued existence of the secondary States, all of which the French Republic is accused of having shapen. Upon these conditions peace is made if you will. Let us make the armistice general for all the armies, and enter into negotiations instantly."

Order to Seize all English in France, Announced in the Moniteur, May, 1803.

"The Government of the Republic, having heard read, by the Minister of Marine and Colonies, a despatch from the maritime prefect at Brest, announcing that two English frigates had taken two merchant vessels in the Bay of Andrieu, without any previous declaration of war, and in manifest violation of the law of nations,—

"All the English, from the ages of eighteen to sixty, or holding any commission from his Britannic Majesty, who are at present in France, shall immediately be constituted prisoners of war, to answer for those citizens of the Republic who may have been arrested and made prisoners by the vessels or subjects of his Britannic Majesty previous to any declaration of hostilities."

VI

NAPOLEON, EMPEROR OF FRANCE.

Letter to the Pope, 1804.

"*Most Holy Father:*—The happy effect produced upon the character and morality of my people by the reestablishment of religion induces me to beg your Holiness to give me a new proof of your interest in my destiny, and in that of this great nation, in one of the most important conjunctures presented in the annals of the world. I beg you to come and give, to the highest degree, a religious character to the anointing and coronation of the first Emperor of the French. That ceremony will acquire a new lustre by being performed by your Holiness in person. It will bring down upon our people, and yourself, the blessing of God, whose decrees rule the destiny of Empires and families. Your Holiness is aware of the affectionate sentiments I have long borne towards you, and can thence judge of the pleasure that this occurrence will afford me of testifying them anew. We pray God that He may preserve you, most Holy Father, for many years, to rule and govern our mother, the Holy Church.

"Your dutiful son,

"Napoleon."

Address to the Troops on Presenting the Colors, Dec. 3, 1804.

"Soldiers: Behold your colors! These eagles will always be your rallying point! They will always be where your Emperor may think them necessary for the defense of his throne and of his people. Swear to sacrifice your lives to defend them, and by your courage to keep them constantly in the path of victory. Swear!"

Letter to the King of England, Jan. 2, 1805.

"*Sir, my brother:*—Called to the throne by Providence, by the suffrages of the Senate, of the people, and of the army, my first desire is peace. France and England, abusing their prosperity, may contend for ages. But do their respective governments fulfill their most sacred duties in causing so much blood to be vainly shed without the hope of advantage or the hope of cessation? I do not conceive that it can be deemed dishonorable in me to make the first advances. I believe it has been sufficiently proved to the world that I dread none of the chances of war, which indeed offer nothing that I can fear. Though peace is the wish of my heart, yet war has never been adverse to my glory. I conjure your Majesty, then, not to refuse the happiness of giving peace to the world. Delay not that grateful satisfaction, that it may be a legacy for your children; for never have arisen more favorable circumstances, nor a more propitious moment for calming every passion and displaying the best feelings of humanity and reason. That moment once lost, what term shall we set to a struggle which all my efforts have been unable to terminate. In the space of ten years your Majesty has gained more in wealth and territory than the extent of Europe comprehends. Your people have attained the height of prosperity. What then has your Majesty to hope from war? The world is sufficiently extensive for our two nations; and reason might assist us to discover means of conciliating all, were both parties animated by a spirit of reconcilement. At all events I have discharged a sacred duty, and one clear to my heart. Your Majesty may rely upon the sincerity of the sentiments now expressed, and on my desire to afford your Majesty every proof of that sincerity."

Conversation with Decier Regarding the Marriage of Jerome Bonaparte, May 6, 1805.

"Jerome is wrong to think that he will be able to count upon any weakness on my part, for, not having the rights of a father, I cannot entertain for him the feeling of a father; a father allows himself to be blinded, and it pleases him to be blinded because he identifies his son with himself.

"But what am I to Jerome? Sole instrument of my destiny, I owe nothing to my brothers. They have made an abundant harvest out of what I have accomplished in the way of glory; but, for all that, they must not abandon the field and deprive me of the aid I have a right to expect from them. They will cease to be anything for me, directly they take a road opposed to mine. If I expect so much from my brothers, who have already rendered many services, if I have abandoned the one who, in mature age (Lucien), refused to follow my advice, what must not Jerome, who is still young, and is known only for his neglect of duty, expect? If he does nothing for me, I shall see in this the decree of destiny, which has decided that I shall do nothing for him."

Letter to Jerome Bonaparte, May 6, 1805.

ALEXANDRIA, 16 Floréal, year 13.

"My brother, your letter of this morning informs me of your arrival in Alexandria. There are no faults that a true repentance will not efface in my eyes.

"Your union with Mademoiselle Paterson is null, alike in the eyes of religion and of the law. Write Mademoiselle Paterson to return to America. I will grant her a pension of 60,000 francs during her lifetime, on condition that she will under no circumstances bear my name,—she has no right to do so owing to the non-existence of her marriage. You must yourself give her to understand that you are powerless to change the nature of things. Your marriage being thus annulled by your own consent, I will restore to you my friendship and continue to feel for you as I have done since your infancy, hoping that you will prove yourself worthy by the efforts you make to acquire my gratitude and to distinguish yourself in my armies."

Address to the Senate, 1805.

"Senators: It is necessary, in the present state of Europe, that I should explain to you my sentiments. I am about to quit my capital, to place myself at the head of my army, to bear prompt assistance to my allies, and to defend the dearest interests of my people. The wishes of the eternal enemies of the continent are accomplished. Hostilities have commenced in the midst of Germany; Austria and Russia have united with England, and our generation is involved anew in the calamity of war. A few days ago I still cherished the hope that peace would not be disturbed. But the Austrian army has passed the Inn. Munich is invaded; the Elector of Bavaria has been driven from his capital. All my hopes of peace have vanished."

Proclamation to the Troops on the Commencement of the War of the Third Coalition, September, 1805.

"Soldiers: The war of the third coalition is commenced. The Austrian army has passed the Inn, violated treaties, attacked and driven our ally from his capital. You yourselves have been obliged to hasten, by forced marches, to the defence of our frontiers. But you have now passed the Rhine; and we will not stop now till we have secured the independence of the Germanic body, succored our allies, and humbled the pride of our unjust assailants. We will not again make peace without a sufficient guarantee! Our generosity shall not again wrong our policy. Soldiers, your Emperor is among you! You are but the advanced guard of the great people. If it is necessary they will all rise at my call to confound and dissolve this new league, which has been created by the malice and gold of England. But, soldiers, we shall have forced marches to make, privations of every kind to endure. Still, whatever obstacles may be opposed to us, we will conquer them; and we will never rest until we have planted our eagles on the territory of our enemies!"

Address to the Austrians, after the Fall of Ulm, October, 1805.

"Gentlemen: War has its chances. Often victorious, you must expect sometimes to be vanquished. Your master wages against me an unjust war. I say it candidly, I know not for what I am fighting, I know not what he requires of me. He has wished to remind me that I was once a soldier. I trust he will find that I have not forgotten my original avocation. I want nothing on the continent, I desire ships, colonies, and commerce. Their acquisition would be as advantageous to you as to me."

Address to the Troops after the War of the Third Coalition, October, 1805.

"Soldiers of the Grand Army: In a fortnight we have finished the entire campaign. What we proposed to do has been done. We have driven the Austrian troops from Bavaria, and restored our ally to the sovereignty of his dominions.

"That army, which, with equal presumption and imprudence, marched upon our frontiers, is annihilated.

"But what does this signify to England? She has gained her object. We are no longer at Boulogne, and her subsidy will be neither more nor less.

"Of a hundred thousand men who composed that army, sixty thousand are prisoners. They will replace our conscripts in the labors of agriculture.

"Two hundred pieces of cannon, the whole park of artillery, ninety flags, and all their generals are in our power. Fifteen thousand men only have escaped.

"Soldiers: I announced to you the result of a great battle; but, thanks to the ill-devised schemes of the enemy, I was enabled to secure the wished-for result without incurring any danger, and, what is unexampled in the history of nations, that result has been gained at the sacrifice of scarcely fifteen hundred men killed and wounded.

"Soldiers: this success is due to your unlimited confidence in your Emperor, to your patience in enduring fatigues and privations of every kind, and to your singular courage and intrepidity.

"But we will not stop here. You are impatient to commence another campaign.

"The Russian army, which English gold has brought from the extremities of the universe, shall experience the same fate as that which we have just defeated.

"In the conflict in which we are about to engage, the honor of the French infantry is especially concerned. We shall now see another decision of the question which has already been determined in Switzerland and Holland; namely, whether the French infantry is the first or the second in Europe.

"Among the Russians there are no generals in contending against whom I can acquire any glory. All I wish is to obtain the victory with the least possible bloodshed. My soldiers are my children."

Proclamation to the Soldiers before the Battle of Austerlitz, Dec. 1, 1805.

"Soldiers: The Russian army has presented itself before you to revenge the disasters of the Austrians at Ulm. They are the same men that you conquered at Hollabrunn, and on whose flying trails you have followed. The positions which we occupy are formidable. While they are marching to turn my right, they must present their flank to your blows.

"Soldiers: I will myself direct all your battalions. I will keep myself at a distance from the fire, if, with your accustomed valor, you carry disorder and confusion into the enemies' ranks. But should victory appear for a moment uncertain, you will see your Emperor expose himself to the first strokes. Victory must not be doubtful on this occasion."

Proclamation after the Battle of Austerlitz, Dec. 3, 1805.

"Soldiers: I am satisfied with you. In the Battle of Austerlitz you have justified all that I expected from your intrepidity. You have decorated your eagles with immortal glory. An army of one hundred thousand men, commanded by the Emperors of Russia and Austria, has been, in less than four hours, either cut in pieces or dispersed. Thus in two months the third coalition has been vanquished and dissolved. Peace cannot now be far distant. But I will make only such a peace as gives us guarantee for the future, and secures rewards to our allies. When everything necessary to secure the happiness and prosperity of our country is obtained, I will lead you back to France. My people will behold you again with joy. It will be enough for one of you to say, 'I was at the battle of Austerlitz;' for all your fellow citizens to exclaim, 'There is a brave man.'"

Address to the Soldiers on the Signing of Peace with Austria, Dec. 26, 1805.

"Peace has just been signed by the Emperor of Austria. You have in the last autumn made two campaigns. You have seen your Emperor share your dangers and your fatigues. I wish also that you should see him surrounded by the grandeur and splendor which belong to the sovereign of the first people in. the world. You shall all be there. We will celebrate the names of those who have died in these two campaigns in the field of honor. The world shall ever see us ready to follow their example. We will even do more than we have yet done, if necessary to vindicate our national honor, or to resist the efforts of those who are the eternal enemies of peace upon the continent. During the three months which are necessary to effect your return to France, prove the example for all armies. You have now to give testimonies, not of courage and intrepidity, but of strict discipline. Conduct yourselves like children in the bosom of their family."

Proclamation to the Soldiers, February, 1806.

"Soldiers: For the last ten years I have done everything in my power to save the King of Naples. He has done everything to destroy himself. After the battles of Dego, Mondovi, and Lodi he could oppose to me but a feeble resistance. I relied upon the word of this Prince, and was gracious toward him. When the second coalition was dissolved at Marengo, the King of Naples, who had been the first to commence this unjust war, abandoned by his allies, remained single-handed and defenseless. He implored me. I pardoned him a second time. It is but a few months since you were at the gates of Naples. I had sufficiently powerful reasons for suspecting the treason in contemplation. I was still generous,—I acknowledged the neutrality of Naples. I ordered you to evacuate the Kingdom. For the third time the House of Naples was reestablished and saved. Shall we forgive a fourth time? Shall we rely a fourth time on a court without faith, honor, or reason? No, no! *The dynasty of Naples has ceased to reign.* Its existence is incompatible with the honor of Europe, and the repose of my crown."

Address to the Senate on Annexation of the Cisalpine Republic, 1806.

"Powerful and great is the French Empire. Greater still is our moderation. We have in a manner conquered Holland, Switzerland, Italy, Germany. But, in the midst of such unparalleled success, we have listened only to the counsels of moderation. Of so many conquered provinces, we have retained only the one which was necessary to maintain France in the rank among the nations which she has always enjoyed. The partition of Poland, the provinces torn from Turkey, the conquest of India, and of almost all the European colonies, have turned the balance against us. To form a counterpoise to such acquisitions, we must retain something. But we must keep only what is useful and necessary. Great would have been the addition to the wealth and the resources of our territory, if we had united to them the Italian Republic. But we gave it independence at Lyons. And we now proceed a step further, and recognize its ultimate separation from the crown of France, deferring only the execution of that project till it can be done without danger to Italian independence."

To the Legislative Body before the Battle of Jena, October, 1806.

"Princes, magistrates, soldiers, citizens, we have all but one object in our several departments,—the interests of our country. Weakness in the executive is the greatest of all misfortunes to the people. Soldier, or First Consul, I have but one thought; Emperor, I have no other object,—the prosperity of France. I do not wish to increase its territory, but I am resolved to maintain its integrity. I have no desire to augment the influence which we possess in Europe, but I will not permit that we enjoy to decline. No State shall be incorporated with our empire; but I will not sacrifice my rights, or the ties which unite us to other States."

Address to the Captive Officers after the Battle of Jena, Oct. 15, 1806.

"I know not why I am at war with your sovereign. He is a wise, pacific prince, deserving of respect. I wish to see your country rescued from its humiliating dependence upon Prussia. Why should the Saxons and the French, with no motive for hostility, fight against each other, I am ready, for my part, to give a pledge of my amicable disposition by setting you all at liberty, and by sparing Saxony. All I require of you is your promise no more to bear arms against France."

Proclamation to the Soldiers before Entering Warsaw, Jan. 1, 1807.

"Soldiers: It is a year this very hour since you were on the field of Austerlitz, where the Russian battalions fled in disorder, or surrendered up their arms to their conquerors. Next day proposals of peace were talked of, but they were deceptive. No sooner had the Russians escaped by, perhaps, blamable generosity, from the disasters of the third coalition than they contrived a fourth. But the ally on whose tactics they founded their principal hope was no more. His capitals, his fortresses, his magazines, his arsenals, two hundred and eighty flags, and two hundred field-pieces have fallen into our power. The Oder, the Wartha, the deserts of Poland, and the inclemency of the season, have not for a moment retarded your progress. You have braved all; surmounted all: every obstacle has fled at your approach. The Russians have in vain endeavored to defend the capital of ancient and illustrious Poland. The French eagle hovers over the Vistula. The brave and unfortunate Poles, on beholding you, fancied they saw the legions of Sobiesky returning from their memorable expedition.

"Soldiers: We will not lay down our arms until a general peace has secured the power of our allies, and restored to us our colonies and our freedom of trade. We have gained on the Elbe and Oder, Pondicherry, our Indian establishments, the Cape of Good Hope, and the Spanish colonies. Why should the Russians have the right of opposing destiny and thwarting our just designs? They and we are still the soldiers who fought at Austerlitz."

To the King of Prussia, Entreating Peace after the Battle of Eylau, February, 1807.

"I desire to put a period to the misfortunes of your family, and to organize, as speedily as possible, the Prussian monarchy. Its intermediate power is necessary for the tranquility of Europe. I desire peace with Russia; and, provided the Cabinet of St. Petersburg has no designs upon the Turkish Empire, I see no difficulty in obtaining it. Peace with England is not less essential to all nations. I shall have no hesitation in sending a minister to

Memil to take part in a congress of France, Sweden, England, Russia, Prussia, and Turkey. But, as such a congress may last many years, which would not suit the present condition of Prussia, your Majesty therefore will, I am persuaded, be of opinion that I have taken the simplest method, and one which is most likely to secure the prosperity of your subjects. At all events, I entreat your Majesty to believe in my sincere desire to reestablish amicable relations with so friendly a power as Prussia, and that I wish to do the same with Russia and England."

Address to the Army on its Return to Winter Quarters on the Vistula, 1807.

"Soldiers: We were beginning to taste the sweets of repose in our winter quarters when the enemy attacked the first corps on the lower Vistula. We flew to meet him. We pursued him, sword in hand, eighty leagues. He was driven for shelter beneath the cannons of his fortresses, and beyond the Pregel. We have captured sixty pieces of cannon, sixteen standards, and killed, wounded, or taken more than forty thousand Russians. The brave, who have fallen on our side, have fallen nobly—like soldiers. Their families shall receive our protection. Having thus defeated the whole projects of the enemy, we will return to the Vistula and reenter our winter quarters. Whosoever ventures to disturb our repose will repent of it. Beyond the Vistula, as beyond the Danube, we shall always be the Soldiers of the Grand Army."

Proclamation to the Soldiers after the Battle of Friedland, June 24, 1807.

"Soldiers: On the 5th of June we were attacked in our cantonments by the Russian army. The enemy had mistaken the cause of our inactivity. He perceived too late that our repose was that of a lion. He repents of having disturbed it. In a campaign of ten days we have taken one hundred and twenty pieces of cannon, seven colors, and have killed, wounded, or taken sixty thousand Russians. We have taken from the enemy's army all its magazines, its hospitals, its ambulances, the fortress of Könisberg, the three hundred vessels which were in that port laded with all kinds of military stores, and one hundred and sixty thousand muskets, which England was sending to arm our enemies. From the banks of the Vistula we have come with the speed of the eagle to those of Niemen. At Austerlitz you celebrated the anniversary of the coronation. At Friedland you have worthily celebrated the Battle of Marengo, where we put an end to the war of the second coalition.

"Frenchmen: You have been worthy of yourselves and of me. You will return to France covered with laurels, having obtained a glorious peace, which carries with it a guarantee of its duration. It is time for our country to live in repose, sheltered from the malignant influences of England. My bounties shall prove to you my gratitude, and the full extent of the love which I feel for you."

Letter to Champagny, Nov. 15, 1807.

"Since America suffers her vessels to be searched, she adopts the principle that the flag does not cover the goods.

"Since she recognizes the absurd blockades laid by England, consents to having her vessels incessantly stopped, sent to England, and so turned aside from their course, why should not the Americans suffer the blockade laid by France? Certainly France is no more blockaded by England than England by France. Why should not Americans also suffer their vessels to be searched by French ships? Certainly France recognizes that these measures are unjust, illegal, and subversive of national sovereignty; but it is the duty of nations to resort to force, and to declare themselves against things which dishonor them and disgrace their independence."

Proclamation to the Spaniards on the Abdication of Charles IV., June 2, 1808.

"Spaniards: After a long agony your nation was on the point of perishing. I saw your miseries and hastened to apply a remedy. Your grandeur, your power, form an integral part of my own. Your princes have ceded to me the rights to the crown of Spain. I have no wish to reign over your provinces, but I am desirous of acquiring eternal titles to the love and gratitude of your posterity. Your monarchy is old. My mission is to pour into its veins the blood of youth. I will ameliorate all your institutions and make you enjoy, if you second my efforts, the blessings of reform, without its collisions, its disorders, its convulsions. I have convoked a general assembly of the deputations of your provinces and cities. I am desirous of ascertaining your wants by personal intercourse. I will then lay aside all the titles I have acquired, and place your glorious crown on the head of my second self, after having secured for you a constitution which may establish the sacred and salutary authority of the sovereign, with the liberties and privileges of the people. Spaniards: Reflect on what your fathers were; on what you are now. The fault does not lie in you; but in the constitution by which you have been governed. Conceive the most ardent hopes and confidence in the results of your present situation; for I wish that your latest posterity should preserve the recollection of me, and say: '*He was the regenerator of our country.*'"

Address to the Legislative Body, before Leaving Paris for the Spanish Campaign, 1808.

"I have travelled this year more than three thousand miles in the interior of my empire. The spectacle of this great French family—recently distracted by intestine divisions, now united and happy—has profoundly moved me. I have learned that I cannot be happy myself unless I first see that France is happy. A part of my army is marching to meet the troops which England has landed in Spain. It is an especial blessing of that Providence which has constantly protected our army, that passion has so blinded the English counsels as to induce them to renounce the possession of the seas, and to exhibit their army on the continent. I depart in a few days to place myself at the head of my troops, and, with the aid of God, to crown in Madrid the

King of Spain, and to place our eagles on the fort of Lisbon. The Emperor of Russia and I have met at Erfurt. Our most earnest endeavor has been for peace. We have resolved to make many sacrifices; to confer, if possible, the blessings of maritime commerce upon the hundred millions of men whom we represent. We are of one mind, and we are indissolubly united for peace as for war."

Letter to the Emperor of Austria, October, 1808.

"*Sire, my Brother:*—I thank your Royal and Imperial Majesty for the letter you have been so good as to write me, and which Baron Vincent delivered. I never doubted your Majesty, but I nevertheless feared for a moment that hostilities would be renewed between us. There is, at Vienna, a faction which affects alarm in order to drive your Cabinet to violent measures, which would entail misfortunes greater than those which are passed. I had it in my power to dismember your Majesty's monarchy, or at least to diminish its power. I did not do so. It exists as it is by my consent. This is a plain proof that our accounts are settled; that I have no desire to injure you. I am always ready to guarantee the integrity of your monarchy. I will never do anything adverse to the important interests of States. But your Majesty ought not to bring again under discussion what has been settled by a fifteen years' war. You ought to avoid every proclamation or act calculated to excite dissension. The last levy in mass might have provoked war if I had apprehended that the levy and preparations were made in conjunction with Russia.

"I have just disbanded the camp of the Confederation. I have sent a hundred thousand men to Boulogne to renew my projects against England. I had reason to believe when I had the happiness of seeing your Majesty, and had concluded the treaty of Presburg, that our disputes were terminated forever, and that I might undertake the maritime war without interruption. I beseech your Majesty to distrust those, who, by speaking of the dangers of the monarchy, disturb your happiness and that of your family and people. Those persons alone are dangerous; they create the dangers they pretend to fear. By a straightforward, plain, and ingenious line of conduct, your Majesty will render your people happy, will secure to yourself that tranquility of which you must stand in need after so many troubles, and will be sure of finding me determined to do nothing hostile to your important interests. Let your conduct bespeak confidence, and you will inspire it. The best policy at the present time is simplicity and truth. Confide your troubles to me when you have any, and I will instantly banish them. Allow me to make one observation more—listen to your own judgment—your own feelings—they are much more correct than those of your advisers. I beseech your Majesty to read my letter in the spirit in which it is written, and to see nothing in it inconsistent with the welfare and tranquility of Europe and your Majesty."

Proclamation to the Soldiers, during the March for Spain, 1808.

"Soldiers: After triumphing on the banks of the Vistula and the Danube, with rapid steps you have passed through Germany, This day, without a moment of repose, I command you to traverse France. Soldiers: I have need of you. The hideous presence of the leopard contaminates the peninsula of Spain and Portugal. In terror he must fly before you. Let us bear our triumphal eagles to the pillars of Hercules. There, also, we have injuries to avenge. Soldiers: You have passed the renown of our modern armies, but you have not yet equalled the glories of those Romans, who, in one and the same campaign, were victorious upon the Rhine and the Euphrates, in Illyria and upon the Tagus. A long peace, a lasting prosperity, shall be the reward of your labors. But a real Frenchman ought not, could not, rest until the seas are open to all.

Soldiers: All that you have done, all that you will do for the happiness of the French people, and for my glory, shall be eternal in my heart."

Summons to M. de Morla to Surrender Madrid, Dec. 3, 1808.

"In vain you employ the name of the people. If you cannot find means to pacify them, it is because you yourselves excited them and misled them by falsehood. Assemble the clergy, the heads of the convents, the alcades, and if between this and six in the morning the city has not surrendered, it shall cease to exist. I neither will, nor ought to withdraw my troops. You have slaughtered the unfortunate French who have fallen into your hands. Only two days ago you suffered two servants of the Russian ambassador to be dragged away and put to death in the streets because they were Frenchmen. The incapacity and weakness of a general had put into your hands troops which had capitulated on the field of battle of Baylen, and the capitulation was violated. You, M. de Morla, what sort of a letter did you write to that general? Well did it become you to talk of pillage—you, who having entered Rousillon in 1795, carried off all the women, and divided them as booty among your soldiers. What right had you, moreover, to hold such language. The capitulation of Baylen forbade it. Look what was the conduct of the English, who are far from priding themselves on being strict observers of the law of nations. They complained of the Convention of Cintra, but they fulfilled it. To violate military treaties is to renounce all civilization—to put ourselves on a level with the Bedouins of the desert. How then dare you demand a capitulation—you who violated that of Baylen? See how injustice and bad faith ever recoil upon those who are guilty of them. I had a fleet at Cadiz. It had come there as to a harbor of an ally. You directed against it the mortars of the city which you commanded. I had a Spanish army in my ranks. I preferred to see it escape in English ships, and to fling itself upon the rocks of Espinosa, than to disarm it. I preferred having nine thousand more enemies to fight, to violating good faith and honor. Return to Madrid. I give you till six o'clock to-morrow evening. You have nothing to say to me about the people, but to tell me that they have submitted. If not, you and your troops shall be put to the sword."

Proclamation to the Spanish People, December, 1808.

"I have declared, in a proclamation of the 2d of June, that I wished to be the regenerator of Spain.

To the rights which the princes of the ancient dynasty have ceded to me, you have wished that I should add the rights of conquest. That, however, shall not change my inclination to serve you. I wish to encourage everything that is noble in your own exertions. All that is opposed to your prosperity and your grandeur I wish to destroy. The shackles which have enslaved the people I have broken. I have given you a liberal constitution, and, in the place of an absolute monarchy, a monarchy mild and limited. It depends upon yourselves whether that constitution shall still be your law."

Letter to the American Minister, Armstrong, 1809.

"The seas belong to all nations. Any vessel, sailing under whatsoever flag, recognized and avowed by her, should be as much at home in the midst of the seas as if she were in her own ports. The flag floating from the mast of a merchant vessel should be respected as much as if it floated from the top of a village spire.

"In case of war between two maritime powers, neutrals should follow the legislation of neither one. Every vessel should be protected by its flag. Every power which violates a flag declares war against the power to which it belongs. To insult a merchant vessel which carries the flag of a power, is the same thing as invading a town or colony belonging to that power. His Majesty declares that he considers the fleets of nations as floating colonies belonging to those nations. In consequence of this principle, the sovereignty and independence of a nation is a property of its neighbors. If a French citizen was insulted in an American port or colony, the Government of the United States would not deny that it was responsible for it. In the same way the Government of the United States must be responsible for the violation of French property on board of a ship or floating American colony; otherwise, this Government, not being able to guarantee the integrity of its rights and the independence of its flag, his Majesty considers the American vessels which have been violated by visits, by taxes, and other arbitrary acts, as no longer belonging to the United States, and as denationalized.

"But whenever the Government of the United States shall order its vessels armed to repulse the unjust aggressions of England, to sustain its rights, against the refusal of this power to recognize the great principle that the flag covers the ship, and against its unjust pretension of searching neutral vessels, his Majesty is willing to recognize them and treat them as neutrals."

Proclamation to the Soldiers before the Battle of Eckmuhl, April, 1809.

"Soldiers: The territory of the confederation of the Rhine has been violated. The Austrian general supposes that we are to fly at the sight of his eagles, and abandon our allies to his mercy. I arrive with the rapidity of lightning in the midst of you. Soldiers: I was surrounded by your bayonets, when the Emperor of Austria arrived at my bivouac in Moravia. You heard him employ my clemency, and swear an eternal friendship. Conquerors in three wars, Austria has owed everything to our generosity. Three times she has perjured herself! Our former successes are our guarantee for our future triumphs. Let us march, then, and at our aspect, let the enemy recognize his conquerors."

Proclamation to the Troops at Ratisbon, April, 1809.

"Soldiers: You have justified my anticipations. You have supplied by bravery the want of numbers, and have shown the difference which exists between the soldiers of Cæsar and the armed rabble of Xerxes. Within the space of a few days we have triumphed in the battles of Thaun, Abersberg, and Eckmuhl, and in the combats of Peissing, Landshut, and Ratisbon. One hundred pieces of cannon, forty standards, fifty thousand prisoners, three bridge equipages, three thousand baggage-wagons with their horses, and all the money chests of the regiments, are the fruits of the rapidity of your marches, and of your courage. The enemy, seduced by a perjured Cabinet, appeared to have lost all recollection of you. His awakening has been speedy; you have appeared more terrible than ever. Lately, he crossed the Inn, and invaded the territory of our allies. Lately, he talked of nothing less than carrying the war into the bosom of our country. Now, defeated, dispersed, he flies, in consternation. Already my advance-guard has passed the Inn. In one month we will be in Vienna."

Address to the Troops on Entering Vienna, May, 1809.

"In a month after the enemy passed the Inn, on the same day, at the same hour, we entered Vienna. Their militia, their levies *en masse*, their ramparts, created by the impotent rage of the princes of the House of Lorraine, have fallen at the first sight of you. The princes of that house have abandoned their capital, not like the soldiers of honor, who yield to circumstance and the reverses of war, but as perjurers haunted by the sense of their crime. In flying from Vienna, their adieus to its inhabitants have been murder and conflagration. Like Medea, they have with their own hands massacred their own offspring. Soldiers: The people of Vienna, according to the expression of a deputation of the suburbs, *abandoned*, *widowed*, shall be the object of your regards. I take its good citizens under my special protection. As to the wicked and turbulent, they shall meet with exemplary justice. Soldiers: Be kind to the poor peasants; to those worthy people who have so many claims upon your esteem. Let us not manifest any pride at our success. Let us see in it but a proof of that divine justice which punishes the ungrateful and the perjured."

Proclamation to the Hungarians, 1809.

"Hungarians: The moment is come to revive your independence. I offer you peace, the integrity of your territory, the inviolability of your constitutions,—whether of such as are in actual existence, or of those which the spirit of the time may require. I ask nothing of you. I desire only to see your nation free and independent. Your union with Austria has made your misfortunes. Your blood has flowed for her in distant regions. Your dearest interests have always been sacrificed to those of the Austrian hereditary estates. You form the finest part of the Empire of Austria, yet you are treated as a province. You have national manners, a national language; you boast an ancient and illustrious origin. Resume, then, your existence as a nation. Have a king of your own choice, who will reside among you, and reign for you alone."

VII

THE FALL OF NAPOLEON.

Address to the Troops on the Beginning of the Russian Campaign, May, 1812.

"Soldiers: The second war of Poland has commenced. The first war terminated at Friedland and Tilsit. At Tilsit, Russia swore eternal alliance with France, and war with England. She has openly violated her oath, and refuses to offer any explanation of her strange conduct till the French Eagle shall have passed the Rhine, and, consequently, shall have left her allies at her discretion. Russia is impelled onward by fatality. Her destiny, is about to be accomplished. Does she believe that we have degenerated? that we are no longer the soldiers of Austerlitz? She has placed us between dishonor and war. The choice cannot for an instant be doubtful. Let us march forward, then, and crossing the Niemen, carry the war into her territories. The second war of Poland will be to the French army as glorious as the first. But our next peace must carry with it its own guarantee, and put an end to that arrogant influence which, for the last fifty years, Russia has exercised over the affairs of Europe."

Address to the Troops before the Battle of Borodino, Sept. 7, 1812.

"Soldiers: This is the battle you have so much desired. The victory depends upon you! It is now *necessary to us*. It will give us abundance of good winter quarters, and a prompt return to our country. Behave as at Austerlitz, at Friedland, at Witepsk, at Smolensk, and let the latest posterity recount with pride your conduct on this day; let them say of you, 'He was at the battle under the walls of Moscow.'"

Letter to Alexander I., Emperor of Russia.

MOSCOW, Sept. 20, 1812.

"*Monsieur, my brother:*—Having been informed that the brother of your Imperial Majesty's Minister at Cassel was in Moscow, I sent for him, and we have had a conversation of some length. I have advised his making my sentiments known to your Majesty.

"The superb and beautiful city of Moscow no longer exists. Rostoptchine gave orders to burn it. Four hundred incendiaries were arrested on the spot, all of whom declared that they had received their orders from the governor and the director of the police; they were shot.

"The fire at last appears to have ceased. Three-quarters of the buildings have been burned, the other quarter remains.

"Such conduct is atrocious and useless. Was its object to make way with some treasure? But the treasure was in caves which could not be reached by the fire.

"Moreover, why destroy one of the most beautiful cities in the world, the work of centuries, for so paltry an end? It is the same line of conduct that has been followed from Smolensk, and has left 600,000 families homeless. The fire-engines in Moscow were either broken or made way with, and a portion of the arms in the arsenal given to malefactors, which obliged us to fire a few shots at the Kremlin in order to disperse them.

"Humanity, the interests of your Majesty and of this great city, required that the city should be confided to me as a trust, since it was exposed by the Russian army. It should not have been left without administration, magistrates, and civil guards. Such a plan was adopted at Vienna, Madrid, and twice at Berlin. We ourselves followed out this plan at the time of the entrance of Sonvarof.

"Incendiaries authorize pillage, to which the soldiers surrender themselves in order to dispute the *débris* with the flames.

"If I imagined for an instant that such a state of affairs was authorized by your Majesty, I should not write this letter; but I hold it as impossible that, with your Majesty's principles, and heart, with the justice of your Majesty's ideas, you could authorize excesses that are unworthy of a great sovereign and of a great nation. While the engines were carried from Moscow, one hundred and fifty pieces of field cannon, 60,000 new muskets, 1,600,000 infantry cartridges, 400,000 weights of powder, 300,000 weights of saltpetre, as much sulphur, etc., were left behind.

"I wage war against your Majesty without animosity; a note from you before or after the last battle would have stopped my march, and I should even have liked to have sacrificed the advantage of entering Moscow. If your Majesty retains some remains of your former sentiments, you will take this letter in good part. At all events, you will thank me for giving you an account of what is passing at Moscow."

Discourse at the Opening of the Legislative Body.

Palais des Tuileries, Feb. 14, 1813.

"I entered Russia. The French armies were constantly victorious on the fields of Ostrono, Polotsk, Mohilef, Smolensk, Moskova, Malo-Yaroslavetz. Nowhere could the Russian armies stand before our eagles. Moscow fell into our power.

"When the Russian borders were forced and the powerlessness of their arms was recognized, a swarm of Tartars turned their parricidal hands against the most beautiful provinces of the empire they had been called upon to defend. Inside a few weeks, in spite of the grief and despair of the unfortunate Muscovites, they set fire to over four thousand of their most prosperous villages, and more than fifty of their most beautiful cities; thus gratifying their ancient hatred, and, on the pretext of retarding our progress, surrounding us by a desert waste.

"But we triumphed over all these obstacles; even the conflagration of Moscow, where, in four days, they destroyed the fruits of the toil and thrift of forty generations, in no way changed the prosperous condition of my affairs. But the rigor of an extreme and premature winter laid the weight of a terrible calamity upon my army. In a few nights everything changed. I met with great losses. My soul would have been crushed beneath their weight had I been accessible to any other feelings than the interest, the glory, and the future of my people.

"At sight of the evils that beset us, England's joy was great. Her hopes knew no bounds. She offered our finest provinces as a reward for treachery. As a condition of peace she proposed the extinction of this beautiful empire; which was in other terms a proclamation of perpetual war.

"The energy shown by my people under such grave circumstances, their devotion to the integrity of the empire, the love they have shown me, have dissipated all these chimeras and have brought our enemies to a more just appreciation of affairs.

"The misfortunes occasioned by the severity of the frosts demonstrated to their full extent the grandeur and solidity of this empire, founded upon the exertions and love of fifty million citizens, and upon the territorial resources of the most beautiful countries in the world."

Address to the Legislative Body, December, 1813.

"I have suppressed your address, it was incendiary. I called you round me to do good—you have done ill. Eleven-twelfths of you are well intentioned, the others, and above all, M. Lainé, are factious intriguers, devoted to England, to all my enemies, and corresponding, through the channel of the advocate Désege, with the Prince Regent, Return to your departments and feel that my eye will follow you; you have endeavored to humble me, you may kill me, but you shall not dishonor me. You make remonstrances; is this a time, when the stranger invades our provinces, and two hundred thousand Cossacks are ready to overflow our country? There may have been petty abuses; I never connived at them. You, M. Renouard, you said that Prince Massena robbed a man at Marseilles of his house. You lie! The general took possession of a vacant house, and my minister shall indemnify the proprietor. Is it thus that you dare affront a marshal of France who has bled for his country, and grown gray in victory? Why did you not make your complaints in secret to me? I would have done you justice. We should wash our dirty linen in private, and not drag it out before the world. You call yourselves representatives of the nation. It is not true; you are only deputies of the departments; a small portion of the State, inferior to the Senate, inferior even to the Council of State. The representatives of the people! I am alone the representative of the people. Twice have twenty-four millions of French called me to the throne—which of you durst undertake such a burden? It had already overwhelmed (*écrasé*) your Assemblies, and your Conventions, your Vergniands and your Guadets, your Jacobins and your Girondins. They are all dead! What, who are you? *nothing*—all authority is in the throne; and what is the throne? This wooden frame covered with velvet? No, I am the throne. You have added wrong to reproaches. You have talked of concessions—concessions that even my enemies dared not ask. I suppose if they asked Champagne, you would have given them La Brie besides; but in four months I will conquer peace, or I shall be dead. You advise! how dare you debate on such high matters (*de si graves interêts*)! You have put me in the front of the battle as the cause of war. It is infamous (*c'est une atrocité*). In all your committees you have excluded the friends of the Government, extraordinary commission, committee of finance, committee of the address, all, all my enemies. M. Lainé, I repeat it, is a traitor; he is a wicked man, the others are mere intriguers. I do justice to the eleven-twelfths; but the factious I know and will pursue. Is it, I ask again, is it while the enemy is in France that you should have done this? But nature has gifted me with a determined courage—nothing can overcome me. It cost my pride much, too,—I made that sacrifice; I—but I am above your miserable declamations. I was in need of consolation, and you would mortify me,—but, no, my victories shall crush your clamors; in three months we shall have peace, and you shall repent your folly. *I am one of those who triumph or die.*

"Go back to your departments. If any one of you dare to print your address, I shall publish it in the *Moniteur* with notes of my own. Go, France stands more in need of me than I do of France. I bear the eleven-twelfths of you in my heart. I shall nominate the deputies of the two series which are vacant, and I shall reduce the legislative body to the discharge of its proper duties. The inhabitants of Alsace and Franche-Comté have a better spirit than you; they ask me for arms. I send them, and one of my aides-de-camp will lead them against the enemy."

Address to the Guard, April 2, 1814.

"Soldiers: The enemy has stolen three marches on us, and has made himself master of Paris. We must drive him thence. Frenchmen, unworthy of the name, emigrants whom we have pardoned, have mounted the white cockade and joined the enemy. The wretches shall receive the reward due to this new crime. Let us swear to conquer or die, and to enforce respect to the tri-colored cockade, which has for twenty years accompanied us on the path of glory and honor."

Speech of Abdication, April 2, 1814.

"The allied powers having decided that the Emperor Napoleon is the only obstacle to the reestablishment of peace in Europe, the Emperor Napoleon, faithful to his oath, declares that he is ready to descend from the throne, to leave Europe, and even to lay down his life for the welfare of his country, which is inseparable from the rights of his son, those of the regency of the Empress, and the maintenance of the laws of the empire."

Farewell to the Old Guard, April 20, 1814.

"Soldiers of my old guard, I bid you farewell. For twenty years I have constantly accompanied you on the road to honor and glory. In these latter times, as in the days of our prosperity, you have invariably been models of courage and fidelity. With men such as you our cause could not be lost;

but the war would have been interminable; it would have been civil war, and that would have entailed deeper misfortunes on France. I have sacrificed all my interests to those of the country. I go, but you, my friends, will continue to serve France. Her happiness was my only thought. It will still be the object of my wishes. Do not regret my fate; if I have consented to survive, it is to serve your glory. I intend to write the history of the great achievements we have performed together. Adieu, my friends. Would I could press you all to my heart." Napoleon then ordered the eagles to be brought, and, having embraced them, he added: "I embrace you all in the person of your general. Adieu, soldiers! Be always gallant and good."

Proclamation to the French People on His Return from Elba, March 5, 1815.

"Frenchmen: The defection of the Duke of Castiglione (Augereau) delivered up Lyons without defense to our enemies. The army, the command of which I had entrusted to him, was, by the number of its battalions, the courage and patriotism of the troops that composed it, in a condition to beat the Austrian troops opposed to it, and to arrive in time on the rear of the left flank of the army which threatened Paris. The victories of Champ-Aubert, of

Montmirail, of Château-Thierry, of Van Champs, of Mormons, of Montereau, of Craonne, of Rheims, of Arcis-sur-Aube, and of St. Dizier, the rising of the brave peasants of Lorraine and Champagne, of Alsace, Franche-Comté and Burgundy, and the position which I had taken in the rear of the hostile army, by cutting it off from its magazines, its parks of reserve, its convoys, and all the equipages, had placed it in a desperate situation. The French were never on the point of being more powerful, and the élite of the enemy's army was lost without resource; it would have found a tomb in those vast plains which it had so mercilessly laid waste, when the treason of the Duke of Ragusa delivered up the capital and disorganized the army. The unexpected misconduct of these two generals, who betrayed at once their country, their prince, and their benefactor, changed the fate of the war; the situation of the enemy was such that, at the close of the action which took place before Paris, he was without ammunition, in consequence of his separation from his parks of reserve. In these new and distressing circumstances, my heart was torn, but my mind remained immovable; I consulted only the interests of the country; I banished myself to a rock in the middle of the sea; my life was yours, and might still be useful to you. Frenchmen: In my exile I heard your complaints and your wishes; you accused my long slumber; you reproached me with sacrificing the welfare of the country to my repose. I have traversed the seas through perils of every kind; I return among you to reclaim my rights, which are yours."

Napoleon's Proclamation to the Army on His Return from Elba, March 5, 1815.

"Soldiers: We have not been conquered; two men, sprung from our ranks, have betrayed our laurels, their country, their benefactor, and their prince. Those whom we have beheld for twenty-five years traversing all Europe to raise up enemies against us, who have spent their lives in fighting against us in the ranks of foreign armies, and in cursing our beautiful France, shall they pretend to command or enchain our eagles?—they who have never been able to look them in the face. Shall we suffer them to inherit the fruit of our glorious toils, to take possession of our honors, of our fortunes; to calumniate and revile our glory? If their reign were to continue all would be lost, even the recollection of those memorable days. With what fury they misrepresent them! They seek to tarnish what the world admires; and if there still remain defenders of our glory, they are to be found among those very enemies whom we have confronted in the field of battle. Soldiers: in my exile I have heard your voice; I have come back in spite of all obstacles and all dangers. Your general, called to the throne by the choice of the people, and raised on your shields, is restored to you; come and join him. Mount the tri-colored cockade; you wore it in the days of our greatness. We must forget that we have been the masters of nations; but we must not suffer any to inter-meddle in our affairs. Who would pretend to be master over us? Who would have the power? Resume those eagles which you had at Ulm, at Austerlitz, at Jena, at Eylau, at Wagram, at Friedland, at Tudela, at Eckmühl, at Essling, at Smolensk, at the Moskowa, at Lutzen, at Wurtchen, at Montmirail. The veterans of the armies of the Sambre and Meuse, of the Rhine, of Italy, of Egypt, of the West, of the Grand Army, are illuminated; their honorable scars are stained; their successes would be crimes; the brave would be rebels, if, as the enemies of the people pretend, the legitimate sovereigns were in the midst of foreign armies. Honors, recompenses, favors, are reserved for those who have served with them against the country and against us. Soldiers: Come and range yourselves under the banners of your chief; his existence is only made up of yours; his rights are only those of the people and yours; his interest, his honor, his glory, are no other than your interest, your honor, and your glory. Victory shall march at a charging step; the eagle, with the national colors, shall fly from steeple to steeple, till it reaches the towers of Notre Dame., Then you will be able to show your scars with honor; then you will be able to boast of what you have done; you will be the liberators of the country! In your old age, surrounded and looked up to by your fellow citizens, they will listen to you with respect as you recount your high deeds, you will each of you be able to say with pride, 'And I also made part of that grand army which entered twice within the walls of Vienna, within those of Rome, of Berlin, of Madrid, of Moscow, and which delivered Paris from the stain which treason and the presence of the enemy had imprinted on it' Honor to those brave soldiers, the glory of their country!"

Proclamation on the Anniversary of the Battles of Marengo and Friedland, June 14, 1815.

"Soldiers: This day is the anniversary of Marengo and Friedland, which twice decided the destiny of Europe. Then, as after the battles of Austerlitz and Wagram, we were too generous. We believed in the protestations and oaths of princes to whom we left their thrones. Now, however, leagued together, they strike at the independence and sacred rights of France. They have committed unjust aggressions. Let us march forward and meet them; are we not still the same men? Soldiers: At Jena, these Prussians, now so arrogant, were three to one; at Montmirail six to one. Let those who have been captive to the English describe the nature of their prison ships, and the sufferings they endured. The Saxons, the Belgians, the Hanoverians, the soldiers of the Confederation of the Rhine, lament that they are obliged to use their arms in the cause of princes who are the enemies of justice, and the destroyers of the rights of nations. They well know the coalition to be insatiable. After having swallowed up twelve millions of Poles, twelve millions of Italians, one million of Saxons, and six millions of Belgians, they now wish to devour the States of the second order among the Germans. Madmen! one moment of prosperity has bewildered them. To oppress and humble the people of France is out of their power; once entering our territory, there they will find their doom. Soldiers: We have forced marches before us, battles to fight, and dangers to encounter; but firm in resolution, victory must be ours. The honor and happiness of our country are at stake! and, in short. Frenchmen, the moment is arrived when we must conquer or die!"

Proclamation to the Belgians, June 17, 1815.

"To the Belgians and the inhabitants on the left bank of the Rhine: The ephemeral success of my enemies detached you for a moment from my empire. In my exile, upon a rock in the sea, I heard your complaint; the God of Battles has decided the fate of your beautiful provinces; Napoleon is among you; you are worthy to be Frenchmen. Rise in a body; join my invincible phalanxes to exterminate the remainder of these barbarians, who are your enemies and mine; they fly, with rage and despair in their hearts."

Napoleon's Proclamation to the French People on His Second Abdication, June 22, 1815.

"Frenchmen: In commencing war for the national independence, I relied on the union of all efforts, of all wills, and the concurrence of all the national authorities. I had reason to hope for success, and I braved all the declarations of the powers against me. Circumstances appear to me changed. I offer myself a sacrifice to the hatred of the enemies of France. May they prove sincere in their declarations, and really have directed them only against my power. My political life is terminated, and I proclaim my son, under the title of Napoleon II., Emperor of the French. The present ministers will provisionally form the council of the Government. The interest which I take in my son induces me to invite the chambers to form, without delay, the regency by a law. Unite all for the public safety that you may continue an independent nation."

Bonaparte's Protest, Written on Board the Bellerophon, August 4, 1815.

"I hereby solemnly protest, before God and man, against the injustice offered me, and the violation of my most sacred rights, in forcibly disposing of my person and my liberty. I came freely on board of the *Bellerophon*; I am not a prisoner; I am the guest of England. I was, indeed, instigated to come on board by the captain, who told me that he had been directed by his Government to receive me and my suite, and conduct me to England, if agreeable to my wishes. I presented myself in good faith, with the view of claiming the protection of the English laws. As soon as I had reached the deck of the *Bellerophon*, I considered myself in the home and on the hearth of the British people.

"If it was the intention of Government, in giving orders to the captain of the *Bellerophon* to receive me and my suite, merely to entrap me, it has forfeited its honor and sullied its flag.

"If this act be consummated, it will be useless for the English to talk to Europe of their integrity, their laws, and their liberty. British good faith will have been lost in the hospitality of the *Bellerophon*.

"I appeal to history,—it will say that an enemy, who made war for twenty years upon the English people, came voluntarily, in his misfortunes, to seek an asylum under their laws. What more striking proof could he give of his esteem and his confidence? But what return did England make for so magnanimous an act? They pretended to hold out a friendly hand to this enemy; and when he delivered himself up in good faith, they sacrificed him."

VIII
NAPOLEON'S WILL.

"Napoleon.

"This 15th April, 1821, at Longwood, Island of St. Helena. This is my Testament or act of my last will.

"1. I die in the Apostolical Roman religion, in the bosom of which I was born, more than fifty years since.

"2. It is my wish that my ashes may repose on the banks of the Seine, in the midst of the French people, whom I have loved so well.

"3. I have always had reason to be pleased with my dearest wife, Maria-Louisa. I retain for her, to my last moment, the most tender sentiments. I beseech her to watch, in order to preserve my son from the snares which yet environ his infancy.

"4. I recommend to my son, never to forget that he was born a French prince, and never to allow himself to become an instrument in the hands of the triumvirs who oppress the nations of Europe; he ought never to fight against France, or injure her in any manner; he ought to adopt my motto: *'Everything for the French people.'*

"5. I die prematurely, assassinated by the English oligarchy and its . . .

"The English nation will not be slow in avenging me.

"6. The two unfortunate results of the invasions of France, when she had still so many resources, are to be attributed to the treason of Marmont, Augereau, Talleyrand, and La Fayette.

"I forgive them—may the posterity of France forgive them as I do.

"7. I thank my good and most excellent mother, the Cardinal, my brothers, Joseph, Lucien, and Jerome, Pauline, Caroline, Julie, Hortense, Catherine, Eugène, for the interest they have continued to feel for me. I pardon Louis for the libel he published in 1820; it is replete with false assertions and falsified documents.

"8. I disavow the *Manuscript of St. Helena*, and other works, under the title of *Maxims*, *Sayings*, etc., which persons have been pleased to publish for the last six years. Such are not the rules which have guided my life. I caused the Duc d'Enghien to be arrested and tried, because that step was essential to the safety, interest, and honor of the French people, when the Comte d'Artois was maintaining, by his own confession, sixty assassins at Paris. Under similar circumstances I should act in the same way."

www.ingramcontent.com/pod-product-compliance
Lightning Source LLC
Chambersburg PA
CBHW031405040426
42444CB00005B/427